Belfast Boy

John Harper

Belfast Boy

Acknowledgements

To the people who have shared my journey with these very personal poems and helped in numerous ways through their support for this project, I say thank you to one and all.

First and foremost, I thank my wife Celia Connor for her unfailing love and encouragement to write *Belfast Boy*. To fellow poet Dr John Gardiner for his comments, suggestions of publishers and unwavering support. To my Kentucky maestro and poetry reader, Bill Brown, who not only read and commented on the poems, but along with his sister, Jeanna Brown, helped provide categories of themes which aided in the final ordering of poems. To Kathy Cope-Hardwick, half a world away in the US, who critiqued my poems with a literary eye. To my daughter, Katie Harper, for reading through my poems and listening: with you, I share my creative spirit. To fellow Belfastian and lifelong friend, Maud Hadden, for her insight and detailed descriptions of what the poems meant to her. And lastly, thanks to David Gilbey for inviting me to recite my Belfast Boy poems at the Art Café: The Curious Rabbit in Wagga Wagga, NSW, Australia.

John Harper
February 2022

Belfast Boy
ISBN 978 1 76109 648 8
Copyright © text Celia Connor 2023
Cover image: Angelfish, Katie Harper;
background, Olwyn Connor-Gantinas

First published 2023 by
GINNINDERRA PRESS
PO Box 3461 Port Adelaide 5015
www.ginninderrapress.com.au

Contents

Preface	7
Belfast Boy	11
Freewheeling	12
Orange Tip	13
Blackberries & Sloe	14
The Hawthorn in Winter	15
Daphnia Safari	16
The Yellow Submarine	18
Bullet the Grey Sky	19
My Da's Shed	20
The Pig	21
Flying Free	22
Bedtime Story	23
Daily Irish Bread	25
Curlew	27
The Road	28
The Dish	29
The Border	30
House Martins	31
Moss	32
Foot Patrol	33
Invisible Son	34
A Spanner…	35
The Grey	37
Red	38
Belfast Day	39
Exhume	40
Portaferry	41
Patterns	42

The Present	43
Whistle	44
Donaghrisk	45
Amnesia	46
Memories With My Dad	47
Dangerous Ground	48
Half Brick	49
Rathlin	50
In Between	51
Hot Toddy	52
The Mournes	54
Reversed	55
Sam	56
The Meeting	57
Tullyhogue	59
The Last Time I Saw My Dad	61
Two Trees	62
The News	63
The Hawthorn Tree	64
Going Home	65
Laughter	66
Intimidation	67
Hound of Hell	68
Long Legs	69

Preface

These poems have been a lifetime in the making. A lifetime filled with love, joy, work, longing and loss. A lifetime that came to an end too soon in between the writing and publishing of this work. So these poems tell John's story, from birth to death and everything in between.

John was born in a Belfast city hospital at 8.15 a.m. on a Sunday morning in 1959. His mother, Iris, said he was born 'just in time for church'. John had a beautiful, sweet and melodic tenor voice, and sang in the local church choir from a young age. Music and poetry were his companions throughout his life, expressions of a rich inner creativity.

John loved his close family as well as his many cousins, uncles and aunts on both sides. During his travels, and even though he was separated from them by half a world, he wrote letters, emails, and cards. In his later years, he had not lived in Ireland for over thirty years, and yet he dreamt more often of home and in his own words he still felt 'that salty Atlantic flowing through my veins and the songs whisper in my mouth, and the smell of moss is always near'.

In 1986, at twenty-seven years old, John emigrated to Australia. By then, he had completed his PhD in botany and was working as a university lecturer and researcher. In his professional life, spanning approximately forty years, he published over sixty scientific papers and was a highly regarded and much-loved educator known for singing and writing poetry to help students learn difficult concepts in science. He won many awards for his teaching and lit up his workplace at Charles Sturt University. Everyone knew when he arrived in the morning: the building was filled with his singing or whistling. Everybody was glad to see him, and he always had time for a chat or a joke. He was generous with his time, his energy and his kindness. His passion and love for learning, teaching and sharing knowledge was inspirational and he changed people's lives for the better.

But *Belfast Boy* is not about that John. It is about the John that he carried within him. The small boy that forever remembered, and held close and quiet, the experiences and memories from his childhood before, during and after the Troubles in Northern Ireland. That boy and his trauma he tried to escape, as many did, and he became part of the Irish diaspora and made a new life in Australia. But he carried the seed with him and eventually it took root and grew, even on foreign soil, and John took his life on 28 April 2022. He was sixty-two years old.

All stories have a beginning, a middle and an ending. This selection of poems is also a triad. The first poems are memories of John's childhood before the Troubles. He describes an early childhood in the back streets and wild places of Northern Ireland 'spent with my sister, brother, and friends, full of adventure, fun, bikes, and imagination'. Poems such as 'Freewheeling' and 'Flying Free' express the simple freedom and escape John found after he saved his first pennies to buy a bike. John's father in all his gruff and humorous splendour features in the poems 'Daphnia Safari', 'The Yellow Submarine', 'My Da's Shed', 'Bedtime Story' and 'Daily Irish Bread'.

In 1969, when John was ten, the Troubles started up again. In these poems he relives the impacts of sectarian violence, the presence of armed security forces, witnessing conflict and the experience of living in daily terror. The never knowing whether members of his family were next. Whether he was next. The violence and fear are suggested in poems such as 'The Pig', 'Curlew', 'The Road' and 'House Martins', and fully realised in the brutality of 'Invisible Son'. Amidst this despair are moments of simple pleasure. John described joy in these times as an 'act of rebellion'. 'Whistle' is a light and joyful look at the ritual of drinking tea with his mother.

The last poems describe his memories of his parents and his Irish home, which remained vivid and clear in his mind. He looks back as an exile in 'Amnesia' and 'The Mournes', trying to come to terms with those traumatic circumstances and the longing for home. In one of the final poems, 'The Hawthorn Tree', John's own longing is expressed as he imagines the tree '…alone and dreams and dreams of home'.

And so, over his last years, John's childhood experiences had started to play constantly in his mind. He wondered at 'the Belfast Boy who is still here feeling devastated and afraid'. Wondering why he is still alive, and when it might be his turn to be taken by a bullet or a bomb. He worked very hard to try and process these traumatic thoughts and feelings and heal. His family, friends and many medical professionals tried to support him, but the past came rushing in, taking him back over and over, and it was just too big for his sensitive soul to manage.

John lit up our world with his beautiful spirit. Now, he has found his last peaceful home in our hearts and there we hold him safe. He will continue to be part of all our lives. John loved to share himself, and it was his hope that this book of poetry would help others to heal and grow through their trauma, no matter where in the world they were. In John's words,

This book is a testament to survival, loss, and joy. It is a tribute and a salute to those who were lost in the Troubles and to those who, as refugees, tumble into other backyards looking for sanctuary and kindness.

And so, we all give thanks for the gifts he gave us in life and the memories we have to hold and treasure. My thanks for a beautiful husband, and to his loving children and stepchildren, Amali, Katie, Liesel, Kester and Olwyn, his brother Tom and sister Karen and all the other family, friends and colleagues who were blessed to be part of his life. And thank you to John from all of us, for being inspirational, funny, gentle, loving, generous …and always kind.

Celia Connor

Belfast Boy

If I could talk to me, ten years old in '69, I would say,
'Find a way not to die inside.'

Freewheeling

for Derek

The thunder of ball bearings
On concrete pavers

A small boy lies flat, flies
Close to the ground

Stomach pounding with
Excitement and fear

The corner of Kell's Avenue
Draws near

Orange Tip

I'm standing in my garden
Look what's in my cupped hands!

A rare butterfly
Its white wings have orange tips

I look at it for a moment
Then set this beauty free

Straight up it flies
Bird plucked from the skies

I cry because it was me.

Blackberries & Sloe

Along Black's Stream I go
Picking blackberries and sloe

The blackberries lush and proud
And some not so

But my mouth after the sweet taste of
Autumn's pride

Puckers with the sour, dry sloe

The Hawthorn in Winter

Skeletal bare-boned thorny
Twisted twigs, gnarled bark

I stand by you in the rainswept
Night as brooding clouds depart

Your branches wave defeated
Silhouettes of what has past

Ghost eyes watching from the ditches
History staring in the dark

Daphnia Safari

My dad kept tropical fish
Huge majestic angel fish
Were his delight

There were also neon tetras,
Harlequins, guppies
Siamese fighting fish, black mollies
Zebras, catfish sucker, tiger barbs…

These are fishes I grew up with
And I loved to watch them but was
More interested in bikes

I remember my dad supplemented
The dried fish food with live tiny white worms
That bred in wooden boxes he made
Fed them on white bread soaked in milk

Put a glass plate over the soil they were in
And they came to the surface.

But the most fascinating food were daphnia!
Commonly called water fleas
My dad kept them in old sinks on top
Of our flat-roofed concrete bunker-shed.

They would breed there but occasionally we
Had to go and get fresh stocks from freshwater ponds
My dad had found a great source in my school.
A flooded pond teeming with them
One night he said, let's go and get some daphnia, son.

So, even though it was dark, off we went, me clinging
To him on the back of his black BSA motorbike
Carrying a home-made net made from my mum's
Old stockings

We climbed over the fence and my dad bent down with the
Net ready to swish it to collect the daphnia
We looked across the pond into the shadowy other side and it moved
This way and that – it was teaming with rats, hundreds of rats!

The Yellow Submarine

My dad bought an 'oul' Vauxhall Victor
As yellow as a sick banana

It drove like a boat under water
So we called it the Yellow Submarine

The leaf springs were slow and spongy
When we went over a bump the car
Rocked and rolled

It couldn't pull the skin of a rice puddin'
But boy that car was gold!

Bullet the Grey Sky

We were playing games in Malinmore
They were plying death in Lenadoon

A stray bullet flew overhead
The whole street looked up

I will never forget that sound
Whizzing through the air

Rubber bullet and live shot on
That day

The memory lingers clear
Never will it
Go away

My Da's Shed

My da's shed was my sanctuary where I would hide away
I would spend hours in there and the key, longer than my hand
Locked the door from the inside.

In this world of wall tools and wooden boxes full of washers, nuts, bolts…
And spaceship-like television valves, I would distract myself
From the world outside

My dad seldom disturbed me
Perhaps he knew how important his shed was to me

The Pig

The Pig was green
From its rear soldiers appeared

Us kids crowded round
In the summer sun

A dog nonchalantly lifted its leg
Yelped from an electric shock

The driver smiled

Flying Free

Flying but firmly
On the ground

The wind cool on my face
Two wheels a blur

Black's Path turn
Anticipating the crunch of cinders

Ride on towards Dunmurry station
Racing a Lisburn train!

'Lady Dixon's' beckons me
On my own, alive and free!

Bedtime Story

Tell me a story
Make it up
As you go
Along

I'll stop you
With questions

Snuggle down
Under the covers

Hear your soothing
Voice in the darkness

The child in the story
Is lost
It's getting dark and
They are far from home
And afraid

Night's cold gathers around
Them
Night noises amplified

They stumble out of a hedge
Onto the road

Fear grips them like a vice
I go further under the covers

A solitary light on the road
Approaches
Fear mingles with hope

A motorbike approaches
Stops
Dad has found you-me
And takes us home

Daily Irish Bread

My father was a baker
His father was one too

He said, 'Son, do well at school
This baking lark's not for you.'

'The days start very early
The work is sweat and toil.'

'A stupid doughy is what
I am.'

'There's no sense of job satisfaction.'
'Study hard, son, be the man!'

I did as I was told as a good boy should
I went to university did the best that I could

I worked there in the summer and did
Some winter nightshifts too

The work was hard and boring
You were right, Dad! Thank you!

And now many years have
Passed
The Oul Doughy has passed too

I came across some of his mixes
Recipes to you

I remember Doughy sayings like
'What's your mix?' and 'Now you're
Cooking with gas!'

But his unique retort – 'Holy Suffering Alec!'
Always made me laugh

So in your honour, from your mixes,
I'm making soda bread, and potato farls

I'll have them with an Ulster fry
With a cardiac ambulance standing by!

Curlew

Above the fields of rushes
I hear a curlew's cry

So hauntingly beautiful
Sweet sadness fills the sky

A car bomb explodes in Belfast
Curved beak slices air

You vanish like a phantom
Death is over there

The Road

I ride my bike on the other side
Past the flowers and cross

Two brother's bodies
Had lain there

I feel desolate, scared, forlorn
Cycle fast as I can up the rain swept
Road

The Dish

I shared a dish with you
I tasted your fear
And then I knew

The turmoil
You had been going
Through

A bitter gift
To be sick
Not eat

To feel that sense
Of helplessness
And defeat

To be paralysed
To be chased by the
Hounds of dread

But I am glad
We have shared these feelings
And smile ahead

Our fears we know
Let's hope our adversities
Melt like summer snow

The Border

The border was at the end of our street
Fifty metres or so from our
Front door
I used to cross over on my bike but not any more
A big steel door is there now
Locked and sealed to keep
'penguins' and 'cats' apart.

House Martins

Mud homes built at the apex of our gable wall
Year after year they would return from Africa to the same mud nest
We would watch and listen in awe as they flew back and forth
Feeding their fledglings
Their pebble-dashed cliff had bullet holes
They still returned
But we left

Moss

A weary cloud rests
on the ground

I'm gently bathed in
its cold embrace

My hair sticks to my head
My face red and damp

I breathe deep the mossy air
Put my hand on the stone's toupee

I pull some sphagnum and smell its earthy tang
And faeries watch me from the blackthorn

Foot Patrol

A line of khaki against the grey
As uncamouflaged as could be

We stopped playing hide and seek
And watched them pass

Nursing their guns like dangerous babies
Mouths pointed at the ground

Invisible Son

In the darkened streets of Belfast
While the rain comes teeming down
I walk invisible, dissolved in the crowd.

Hypervigilant I search the faces looking
For malevolence in a stare
Watching for something not quite right
Everywhere.

Shopping becomes a gamble, a risk
A defiance. I trust in my guardian angel
To keep me safe and see me to the sanctuary of my home.

But that is not what awaits everyone.
Poor innocents slaughtered.
A bomb in a car, shop or bar,
Slashes lives asunder.
Those left alive wear the indelible
Physical and emotional scars.

I am an invisible son of Ireland
Now forever on the run.

A Spanner…

'Pass me the
How's your father'

You've asked that question
Again!

You're underneath fixing
Our oul car

I guess what did you expect for
50 quid?

'Which spanner do you want?'
I ask your protruding legs

I look into an oil stained canvas bag
Willing one to give me a clue

And then I hear 'Seven-eighths!'
My anxiety grows

I want to do my best but I look at the mix of spanners in the bag and know
7/8 will be hiding at the bottom

So I begin my futile frantic search
Spanners set out on the road

Then out pops your face from under the
Car, you look like you've swallowed a toad!

'Let me look for the 'cursid thing'
You grab the bag from me

Then two minutes later it pisses down
and we both run inside for tea!

I snatch up the canvas bag and in the house
We find there is no 7/8 there at all; it's in the shed!

Oh how I dreaded those
Times!

The Grey

The grey Land Rover
Moves slowly up our
Street

Skirts pulled down
To prevent anything
Being rolled underneath

Headlights and windows
Shielded

Moves on not stopping
Watching us self-consciously play

Red

When they slaughtered pigs at Colin Glen
Black's Stream would run red with their blood

The look and the smell
Clings to my memory

I hear the squealing, an echo loud and clear
So much blood and so much fear

Belfast Day

I walk through the mist-shrouded botanic gardens
In the wee hours
From a student party

Cold drips from the trees
Street lights glimmering sickly orange

The white dome of the palm house
Looms a dinosaur's ribcage

A scared defiant shadow in the dangerous moonlight
I walk towards the locked gate

Clumsy black cat slinks over and melts into the Holy Land
Towards College Park Avenue

I approach my grandparents' house
Standing anonymous, shoulder to shoulder
A silent giant in a line-up

Safe inside I climb the stairs
Three flights to the top room
Curse the creaking floorboards

I hear the grandmother clock marking time

And the thin wet light comes through my window.

Exhume

I have a recurring dream
Where I have murdered
Part of me, buried somewhere
In a dell under a hawthorn tree.

And I go there in fear and exhume
What's lying there, and discover it
Is the part of me that I'm afraid to
Share.

Not that it is a monster or something
That brings me shame but It has
Been hidden for so long it feels that
It is wrong.

Portaferry

The air is crisp, cold, fresh
Low clouds scud by

I walk towards the ferry
As cars drive on board

I stand on the deck
the menacing current swirls

I watch the turning tide rushing
Bottleneck through Strangford lough

I see the small green tussocky
Pockmarked islands

I smoke an invisible cigarette
It starts to rain

I retract inside my duffel coat
Hermit crab in softshell

I think of hot clam chowder
As Strangford moves closer

I foresee stout by the turf fire
And craic at the end of
The day

Patterns

Don't go home the same way twice
Don't form patterns

Don't get noticed
Don't leave things to chance

Don't be visible
Don't be seen

The Present

A Christmas
Atlantic wind
Steam issues
From the Crown

I am birthed to
The icy Belfast
Night with smoke
And sweat

The night bites but the
Street is alive
With lights
Cars buses
Coloured trees!

I walk on up the
Road then a colder
Fear hits me

I have left a
Package!

Whistle

From the kitchen I hear the pots and pans clang
percussion played in time to your joyful whistle

The mundane tasks are tasks no more, your soul it shines,
My heart it soars
I come down the stairs and there you are

You smile and say,
'Would you like a wee cup of tea, son?'

And although you're gone many's a year,
In my mind and in my ear

I hear your whistle loud and clear
And I drink tea with you once more

Donaghrisk

Sacred Circle of stone
Embrace Aunty Kitty &
Her mother's
Bones

Two sentinel yew trees
Make an archway
To the beyond

Unreadable headstones
Tumble
Snowdrops blossom on
The graves

The vault broods
Slits in the walls let
The air in

Decayed coffins in
The alcoves
It starts to rain
Cold and biting

The discontented
Winter wind disturbs
The yew

I take a quartz stone
From their grave
And part of me
Stays
In exchange

Amnesia

I had forgotten who I really was
Because I had run away.
It seemed that there was the cloak of death everywhere.
Every day.
The rain, the grey, mirrored the feelings inside.
My dreams had turned to black.
So I went as far as I could go and thought
There was no going back.

But though I have been away now
Longer than I have been there
I feel the land is calling to me and others from far away.
'Come back,' she cries. 'I need you and the other lost souls too.
For you are part of me and I am part of you.'
So if you want to discover who you really are,
Your stolen voice must return and echo in the hills of home.

Memories With My Dad

A blue box kite flies up to touch
The sky
We send messages up along the twine
The wind pushing it from below

Imagination – science fiction a passion
Shared with us
Robots, alien worlds, Interstellar flight
Asimov, Clarke, Wyndham…

Antidisestablishmentarianism!
Nomenclature plus
A dictionary ready to be looked up
Questions, answers

A rare strap that we deserved!
Lots of laughs, love and support
Good memories

A dinosaur lurching cross contemporary landscapes

Belfast's Alf Garnet
A booming voice
Singing 'I believe'
But you didn't

Drunken conversations
The armour exposed
Love shining out
A fading light
A wisp on the breeze

Dangerous Ground

Love does not listen to your banging drum
Your tribal chants or what you think of as fun

Love draws me like a moth to your arms
Over no-man's-land onto dangerous ground

Where the postboxes have been changed from 'stop' to 'go'
Do I look out of place, does my 'colour' show?

My heart pounds in my throat as I approach your door
Fear and excitement a wild mixture for sure!

Half Brick

Stones and half bricks
Lie on the road and pavement

Spent weapons from yesterday
A half brick stained with blood.

I look away trying not to see
But do anyway.

Rathlin

An exile there on Rathlin
A dog leg in the sea

Where the puffins cling
To the basaltic cliffs
And Scotland looks at me

Where the boatman is the
Tour guide, drives the van
And keeps the shop

We walk along the 'highway'
And the rain it never stops

In Between

Caught between the spirit world and this hard reality.

Mind floating, shadows move in my periphery.

As the darkness shroud once more covers me
I plead for a dreamless night of sanctuary.

But the demons crawl across the rooftops down the blocked chimney.

And I hear their snarling across the room as my pillow cowers with me.

Anxiety builds like a dam of air and my chest screams mercy.

And an angel comes and lets me sleep
Chasing dark thoughts from me.

Hot Toddy

Taxidermist head
Cotton wool inside.

Through my bleary vision
I see a twinkle in your eye.

'Would you like a wee hot
One, son?' The inevitable question
Comes.

And how can I refuse your gift
Dad? Made with such pride and love.

A measure of Irish whiskey
Black Bush was the best.

Poured into a glass this amber fluid
Would sit there waiting for the rest.

A metal spoon was placed in the glass to conduct the coming heat.

Boiling water was next poured in
Followed by something sweet

Sometimes honey or a teaspoon of sugar as I recall,
Sinking like gems in a golden fall

The mixture was stirred gently then with cloves and a slice of lemon

This was presented to me with a grin followed by the usual sermon

'It may not cure you,' I hear you say
'But it will ease your cause

And I believe a wee hot toddy will kick the cold virus in the balls!'

The Mournes

I stand in my mind's eye
Looking up at thee

The Mountains of Mourne
Sweeping down to the sea

Percy French what an artist
Your words enthral me

Those basaltic beauties
where I long to be

With the exiled I stand where
I've always been

Oh, Mountains of Mourne
I'm mourning for thee

Reversed

My dad had a minor stroke
about ten years before he died.
He lost weight and confidence.

I returned home that Christmas
And there he stood in the kitchen
One night confused and afraid.

I turned to him, gently
held his hands,
looked into his faded blue eyes
and said, 'It's all right, Dad.'

He looked back into mine
and I felt the tension go.
I thought of how as a child
my dad consoled me.

And now our roles were
reversed.

Sam

There was a teacher in my secondary school
A giant man tall as a tree and balding
His name was Sam

He was a beautiful human
Treated us kids like we were important
Taught us with kindness and humour

He taught biology
Spoke with an English accent
Had a smile as wide as a mile

He inspired me to be a teacher
So I studied hard and went to
University

I now teach biology at university
And Sam's way of teaching is fundamental
to what I do

The years passed and I always wanted
To thank him and let him know how much
His teaching meant to me

But I was in Australia
He passed away last year

The Meeting

You know there are things in life that happen to you
And you say to yourself
Was that divine intervention,
Or did my wish just get granted?

I remember one such event with clarity
And it brings a tear of gratitude when I think about it

My favourite teacher at secondary school, Sam, taught biology
A pattern-baldness tree of a man with a heart that was as big as he

He taught us with humour and kindness and I knew he really cared
He towered above us all but was right down there with us

I studied biology at university
And now teach it to hundreds of students, thanks to Sam

The years passed and I wished that I could tell him
How much he meant to me
And how he had inspired me and what a wonderful
Difference he had made

But I was in Australia and he was back in Ireland
And I thought it's never going to happen

It happened! I was home for two weeks,
Standing in an insurance brokers in Bachelors Walk
Getting temporary insurance for my dad's car
When I looked out the window…

There Sam stood, about to get into his car.
He bent down and tall as he was hit his head
On the top of the door

The moment had come!
I walked outside and held out my hand, we spoke briefly

In those precious moments I told him what his teaching
Had meant to me
He said he didn't know that he had made any difference
And I said 'You did good!'

I can still see the wave of emotion that came over him,
I can still see the mist
He mumbled something and I smiled and we parted
And I am forever grateful.

Tullyhogue

I walk under
The shadows
Of the circle
Trees

The green dappled
Light through the
Beech

Dances on my
Face

The stream
Clear and
Pure
Chats away

The stones
Listen
The moss
Glistens

The smell
Of the damp

Earth, leaves
Sweet decay

And I rejoice
To be

And I see you
There my
Mother

Bathed with
Golden light

One last glimpse
Of your first home
Before you take
Flight

On the wings of
Our
Love

The Last Time I Saw My Dad

The smell of concentrated urine and faeces nearly
Knock me off my feet

You look at me with a wild stare when I tell you I am going to
Get the nurse to clean you up

'You will not!' This defiant voice from a shadow breaks my heart
'Why?' I ask. 'Because I'm telling you!'

I go anyway and come back later when you are clean
But you are asleep

I sit beside you, stroke your long white hair that you
Refuse to get cut
Tell you 'I love you' and say 'Goodbye.'

Your skeletal frame sunken cheeks
I barely recognise you

I buy flowers for the nurses as a token of my gratitude
Their dedication and care gives me comfort
You are well looked after

They try so hard to get you to eat to take your tablets

But you stand on a hill alone fist raised in the air
Shouting 'Grim Reaper, where are you?
Come and get me, I am done!'
And he comes.

Two Trees

If you look on Google Street
Where our house used to be

Standing in its place are two
Trees

Both evergreen, standing side
By side

Branches raised in celebration
To the skies

And my father loved
Trees and my mother loved us all

And I think 'These trees are you.'

The News

I don't watch or listen to the news
But it gets to me anyway

Snatches of hushed conversations in the shops
Friends and enemies in the street talk

There is really no way to get away from it
It pervades your very being

And you know that as much as you don't want to know
You must

The Hawthorn Tree

There is a hawthorn tree
Outside my door

Thoughts of Ireland held
In its red berries

Like a diasporic symbol it
Stands alone and dreams
And dreams of home.

Going Home

River running
Wild and free

White water
Splashes
Pushes back
Against the
Rocks

Leaping high
Ancient urges
Driving me

A salmon
Coursing
From the sea

Laughter

Punched in the face
Kicked when down

Mohammed's jaw was broken
In Belfast town

Violence for the sake of it
Predators in a car

Evil laughter
Cold and sour

Intimidation

We know where you live!
What school do you go to?

Is that a joke or is death
Knocking at your door?

Do I take it seriously?
Or do I laugh it off?

Ignore at your peril
Even if it is not true

In these
Troubled times

Intimidation leads to
Nothing good

One day here
The next day gone

Moved quickly to a
Safer place, for now

Moved on

Hound of Hell

It pursued me down through the years.
It's rasping breath, dank fur of fear.

I put my head down and ran
With tears streaming deep inside.

I heard it baying when someone died.
Needless killings it barked with pride.

I felt it ripping me up inside so
I ran and ran and ran.

But now I know that I must turn,
And face my enemy although I may burn.

And as the flaming hell dog snarls,
A Phoenix cleansed I'll rise.

Long Legs

A daddy-long-
Legs flew into
My room

Around the ceiling
And walls it
Danced

I watched it for
A while with its
Strange loping
Grace

Before gently catching
It and sending it out
Into the cool night

Memories of
My summer
Childhood

Running through
The fields

Daddy long
legs
Flying into my
Face

Tickling
Sunshine days

In the green
Fields of
My first
Home

www.ingramcontent.com/pod-product-compliance
Lightning Source LLC
Chambersburg PA
CBHW071033080526
44587CB00015B/2593